Wet Pain

Claire Rose

BookLeaf
Publishing

Presentation by *BookLeaf Publishing*

Web: www.bookleafpub.com

E-mail: info@bookleafpub.com

ISBN: 9789358737424

First edition 2024

To New York City

"Some people never go crazy. What truly
horrible lives they must lead."

Charles Bukowski

Allow yourself to cry.

Assassin

Today I woke a silent assassin
In velvet gloves
Walking through the rooms of my heart
Killing all the parts of me that can't live without you

August in New York
The hot rain of New York in August hits my skin
Mixing with the tears
My bleeding heart leaves a metallic taste
Reminding me of the salty essence of you - our last
morning - in my mouth

In the doorway
As I quietly close the door
You stand there, on my mind
Keeping watch
Loving thief, having robbed me of my inner peace
Will you ever come back?
Will I?

The L train
I am just another passerby on the streets of New York
Just another crazy girl crying on the L train
Slowly moving towards 3am
Over the Williamsburg bridge, deeper into Brooklyn
Sobbing quietly...
So the Puerto Rican nearby stays asleep
I hope he won't miss his stop

Hunger

No man can eat you out so good
and so completely as grief
It was your undoing of me
That turned me into a woman
you always accused me of being
When I'm good I'm good
When I'm bad I'm better
You only have yourself to blame
Sadness has a flavor
It is an acquired taste

Ménage à trois, New York style
The wildest threesomes I have been having lately
with regret and sadness
Depression joins us time to time
It is a real debauchery then
I wake up destroyed and unable to move
My sleepless nights with invisible lovers

Victim
I am hoping to nail this victim inside me,
once and for all
To the cross of this paper
Typing away in the early hours,
to leave it all behind for good
For the past to sweep away the clutter of days gone by
The hour between dog and wolf
My cat faithfully curled up in my lap
Her weight quietly assuring me
that I am not completely alone
Till the dawn
It's all it comes down to sometimes

Litigator

I do not wish to be right
I simply want to be loved
Can you do that?
And if not, can you let me go?
Or will we spend a lifetime in the court of toxic love?
You say you knew the verdict all at once
The second that we met. GUILTY!
But you went along, backwards, for the ride,
just to prove it?
Which renders YOU crazy. I do not believe it. I CAN'T
You are too logical for THAT anyway
No innocent person willingly enters prison
You are the devil AND the advocate
I LOVE you. Disprove it. YOU CAN'T
Do you enjoy arguing
with what has no shape no form or interest in negotiation
so you do not have to face your own inability
To speak the language of the heart
The only one worth knowing and impossible to teach
Why do you war on what you want the most?
Are you going to have us sentenced both, for good
In the hell called home? Together, apart
Arguing about why this cannot be. ETERNALLY

The odds
You and Me

Warning signs
Why is it, that women tend to ignore red flags
Speeding into the relationship
While men fail to notice the final warning signs
Of a woman about to break it off
How is it we don't see
We choose not to see
What could have saved us so much trouble
And maybe even the connection itself
Love is not blind
Love has its eyes wide open

What I see
I look around and see people so terrified of love
They will rather enter a headlock
or a cul de sac
To avoid taking a chance on something real
I look around and see people so scared
Of the possibility to win
That they'll pick a certain loss
Over uncertainty

Covid 19

As the city shuts down for quarantine
I can't but wonder
That way worse and deadly still
Is to catch the kind of feelings I had for you
The most dangerous thing

Autumn in New York
I fell for you
Like a shooting star
Across the Manhattan sky

I blame it on September light
Bouncing off the steel and glass
Wrapping us in magic of the possibility
To start something anew
On this Harvest Moon

Too little too late
I still cry bitter tears in early hours
When I can't sleep
Not because you didn't love me
But because I didn't love myself enough
To walk away
I chose you every time
For way too long
Until the end…

The best I've ever had that I've never had
You invite me for a meeting
at your loft in Tribeca
The steak is a bit too cooked
Then you make a move
I excuse myself;
I don't want to cheat on my philandering boyfriend
"I must have misread the situation" you say
"Do you mind if I make myself comfortable?"
I sit there, mesmerized, watching you undress
You look me in the eyes when you come
While holding my hand
I get up to leave
Fully clothed
Untouched
Wet
Longing for what I'd just turned down

Sometimes the bravest choice is surrender.

Titanic

We only ever touched the tip
The tip of an iceberg
The iceberg of our love
We never saw more than its sharpest edge
In the blaze of lust
But then again, what goes up must come down
Sun is no exception
It melted the ice and snow as days went by
Till there was nothing left
But a flood of resentment and fears to mop up
Some trips are a once-in-a-lifetime-thing
Like Titanic

Trust
Some people say "trust"
And what they mean is getting a key
to the lock of your freedom
So that they feel safe
On the back of your imprisonment
inside their insecurities
Some people will try to hold you responsible
for how they feel
Do not step into that trap
Set you both free
Stay and do your thing

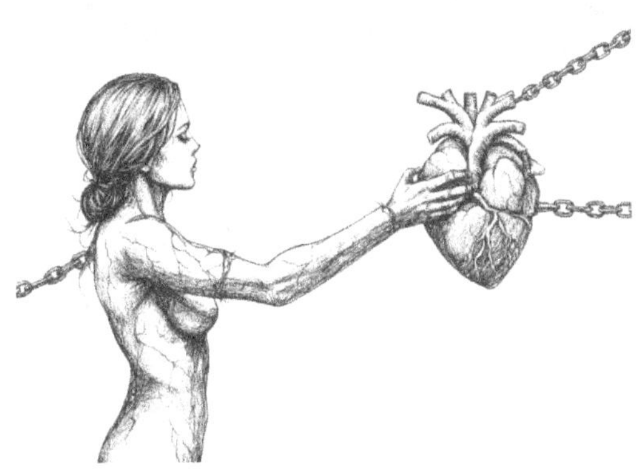

Equality feels like oppression to the privileged.

Risky Business
A man can risk a marriage
His money
His life
His everything
For a moment of desire
For a woman - And yet not love that woman
He can risk it all – for her body -
and still despise her spirit
Desire is not love
To be lusted after does not equate to being cherished
We tell little girls about the importance of being pretty
No sooner than they walk
They learn that the value of a woman
Is according to her desirability
The greatest betrayal of all
In the end most men commit to the safe, reliable
respectable girl next door
And lust after the ones who turn heads
Behind their good girls' backs
Both women crying in the corner
The men restless
So long the vagina rules the world
While deemed dirty and dangerous
The world will be a tricky place to navigate for all
Tell your daughter, that the greatest thing
A man can give
Is not a compliment
But respect for all that she is
And his time

Fall

I lie quietly in my bed
The late morning sun streaming in
Lazy
I listen to the season change
One more time, yet again
Through the open window
the breeze reaches out to my naked skin
and licks it clean
I let it happen and chime in, with my imagination
Inviting you back, even if for an hour
Or maybe two
Thinking of your fingers digging gently
into my inner thigh
As you look up and your eyes meet mine
When you go down on me
I ascend towards the stars
Above the SoHo sky
It all fades into white

Tragedy

How tragic to look in the mirror
and think "This is all I have"
This fallacy that works so well
for the dominance of one species
For women to believe that their worth
is out of their control
Predestined to go down with time
This hilarious denial of depth and value
of anything beyond skin
Directly linked to the lies about the filth of the body
And its purpose
"But of course you want kids"
I want pleasure
And an enigmatic life
And I know there is so much more to me
Than being an arm candy or just a vessel
For a man's gene pool legacy

The third person
He's growing old with her
You're aging with him
Be mindful of that distinction

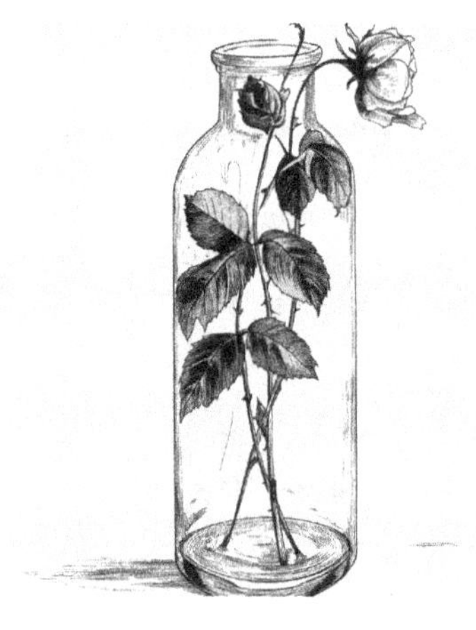

Pride
Cut me with your anger
Find that I bleed honey
Cruelty is the first defense of the weak
So go on
Find my Achilles heel
and prove that you're a man
Take it out on me
The wife you could never please
The women who mopped the floor with you
Chewed you up and spat you out
Tell me all about it
Coz you're oh so much better than me
And all the rest of us

Scared Lovers' Remorse
In the end it is those who held back
That are left with the greatest remorse
The ones trying to avoid getting hurt
Experience the greatest pain
When they find that heart is meant to break
Time and again
For that is how we learn
That is how we grow
Whoever held on to their upper hand
Stayed in control
Cheated themselves into regret

Anxiety
We are not human doings
We are human beings
Alone and terrified
Of all the demons inside your head
The things we learn to hide
behind the business of each day
The running and hustling
Worry not
Sit down and look in the mirror of self
Discover, breath by breath
You are a daughter of The Universe
How could you be ugly?

Void
Someone's absence can be the greatest presence felt
It can be the place someone didn't fill
The gaping void left unclaimed
That will take over the crowded room

The Price
The essence of the rose is known by its thorn
He who fears within goes without
Some people know the cost of everything
and value of nothing

Sleeping with the enemy
I know prejudice
Some people wear it like an invisible cloak
A hallmark on their mind
A little blue chip the society inserted
"For your comfort, for your own good"
Before you could remember
Your own innocence
I smell it in your sweat and I taste it in your cum
It's not cute
Your sense of entitlement
Based upon your place of birth
And language that your parents used –
not in a loving way
Your mummy issues written all over you
You do not get to hurt me with your faith
The world as we know it is crumbling
That is what you made it – unsustainable
I will not be buried under the rubble
of your anger and pent-up angst
You do not get to make me small
I've walked much further than you ever dared
You are the one being left behind
The new is coming into the world
Birthed by the desire to merge and belong
Not because of a passport
But based upon the songs of the soul
How should we treat others?
There is no other.

Heart is a weapon size of a fist.

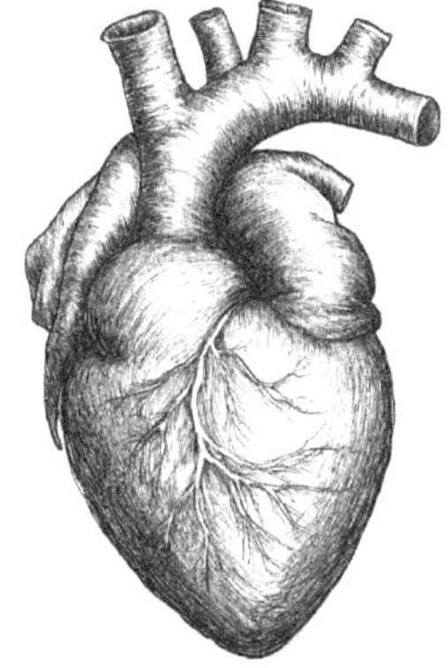

.

Between a rock and a hard place
I want you to be demure you say
But sexy, so everyone is jealous
I want you to be 20 years younger, you say
But my equal
I want you to shine you say
But not brighter than me
I want you to work you say
But mainly around my schedule
I want you to be a Madonna you say
But a whore as well, for good measure
I want you to be impressive you say
But very humble, know your place!
I want you to speak up you say
But not when I have not prompted you
I want you to understand you say
But I won't explain myself
I want you to tell me everything you say
But I don't have time to listen
I want you to have opinions you say
But not different to mine
I want you to achieve you say
But really not too much
I want you to pursue your dreams you say
But not if it's my nightmare
I want you to be yourself you say
But change now

Situationship
You take me out but can't meet my eyes
"No stargazing today" you'd say
Why?
Surely not guilt
You don't owe me fidelity
You don't owe me anything
I only want you, fully, when I see you
Isn't it precisely why this should work?
Freedom?

As you duck and cover through the dinner time
I wonder of your lost home, lost nation, lost everything
I wonder of the man you were before
Before New York City and the one before that
Who you were when you spoke your mother tongue
And the air was filled with spice
You fly me on the magic carpet

Laid down on the floor of your Chelsea studio
Large mirror facing the bed
You cook me an amazing breakfast
Things flown in from across the ocean
"Do you like pickle?" Yes, I answer truthfully
You give me an extra one
I feel your thoughts circling around us
"I will be more careful to let more of my walls down with
you"
you conclude

But you cannot, instead you add some insulation
We can't feel anything without feeling everything
I understand it is easier to keep it all sealed tight

Memories of you smell Like Tom Ford's Black Orchid
And taste of Seedlip spiked with rosewater

2020 perfect vision
You couldn't be The One
But for the time being, you were the only
For no good reason the change of season
washed all over me
You were like a holy vision
A scorpion on the prowl
You'd won but you're crying
Anger becomes sorrow
There's no more love to borrow
Should have seen it coming, baby
You're a hunter in the dark
Hindsight is a bitch, my darling
And fire needs a spark

You blew my mind
How could someone so magnificent and so deep
Be so shallow
Fake lips, fake tits and fake personality
Here you are
Running around
Talking about self-mutilation being sexy
You lost my trust before we began
No wonder that we ended
We were not the right fit
I'm wild and dripping with real life
You tell me about fucking the sad Barbie doll
Who can't go to a house party
without the batteries of snow up her nose
Frigid, only money turns her on
What internal massacre happened to you
to be into that?

Girl Math
You look in the mirror
And do the calculations
How long do you have left
To catch the man who counts
Who can pay your life
A beautiful perishable
Desperately hoping to leverage
your assets before they go down
Bargaining with men
Who make their fortunes in trading equity
Despair and insecurity cheapen women
Girls for sale everywhere in New York
How lucky am I
To never have thought myself beautiful

Girl Math II

The men are a list of groceries
You list in no particular order
The school he went to
Harvard or maybe Yale
(Could forgive him Columbia)
The car he drives (Tesla at least)
The money he makes
The zipcode
The penthouse
The house in The Hamptons
The age
The height
The colour of his eyes
The six pack or the lack of thereof
What he lacks in stamina
he makes up for in cash
Stop already, sister
Or don't complain
When you are traded
For the newer model
Men aren't stupid or without any feelings
Contrary to the popular belief
They already did the math as well
They see a woman whose value
Goes down with every breath she takes
In the world of grocery lists and numbers

BJs
You always loved the way I'd suck your cock
And lick it too
Like no one else before you'd say
It would make me proud and sad
I wish they had all loved you like I do
You'd have been better off for it
Softer
To me and you

Women are tested when they have nothing.
Men are tested when they have everything.

Ache
I woke up painfully aware of the hollow part of me
Aching for you to fill me up
Today the depth of me whispered
"Please come"
Quickly
I can't take this
My longing for bliss calling your name
From the very core of me

Middle Age
Can men who never grew up suffer a midlife crisis?
You're too young-looking and juvenile to hit that mark
I must be mistaken
You're almost a quarter of a century older
But acting like it's the other way around
"I'm growing out of your dating group" I'd complain
Year after year you date the same girl
The names and bodies change,
As they come and go
(Sometimes literally)
Replaced one after the other
They spend a little while
Then leave when it's time to get serious
Because you can't
You break the Red Queen Law
It's not that I have wrinkles
It's not any visible changes to my body
It is the expansion that occurred
And I am leaving you behind
I've gotten into a developmental elevator
And you're fighting to stand still
We push each other's buttons

Men capable of handling a woman's past never ask
about it.

Lady Godiva
And if I shall go to hell
I won't walk
I shall be riding a white stallion
Naked, of course
To honor the God in whose image I'd been made
And which offends you so much
There is nothing life given
To leave unexplored
The only hell are other people as we all shall know
Your trying to shame me for myself won't work
I've no guilt left for you to weaponize
I am a Goddess
A Valkyrie
A Queen
I never wanted to be a saint
That was your intention
A trap
So you can watch me fail
Well I have news for you
Saintly women Heaven on Earth don't make
I will keep my sinful ways - my strut
Keep on screaming something 'bout a slut
Well done my boy, well done
Blaming a woman for her nature given gifts

IT doesn't get better
YOU do

Lunatic Love

It comes and goes in waves
My love for you
Like a tide depending on moon's swell
Sometimes it is gone and I am a little bit more free
Other times I am swimming in it up to my neck and more
Sometimes I let myself be madly in love with you, still
You didn't want me and that's ok
I stand by my choices
Despite everything it was you. Or maybe because of it?
I never met an addict who loved needles but hated heroin
All this time. Everytime. Forevertime.

Whiplash
My heart is a handicapped wild horse
I am gently breaking in
Be patient. Use sugar more than stick
I'll give you a ride of your life
Like never before
Or after… The best you ever had you'd say

Sex always hurts or heals
To let someone who doesn't see you
enter your body
is self-harm
These cuts go deeper than a razor ever could
To let someone enter your body
while they deny your spirit
is trauma bonding in motion
To let someone have your body
while they avoid meeting your soul
is denying the very existence of yourself
It is not surprising that most people
in the western world
are behaving like they suffer from some kind of PTSD
Because they do

Friendzone
You never leave me not dancing
Is this what it's supposed to be like?
As I keep you at arm's length
But let you hold me for a heartbeat longer
When we say goodbye
Just friends just friends
The safe refrain of keeping what's best for me at bay
Why on Earth is it so hard to accept
That at the heart of a healthy relationship is friendship
And not an adrenaline driven toxic high
of familiar drama
You never leave me not dancing

Old habits die hard
And lie harder
It is a fool's mistake to be alone
With someone you shouldn't have loved
Into the furtherness of the night

Beware of a man
Who is terrified to elevate a woman
He will surely take her down

Sometimes
Hope is a tease
The most dangerous thing
Keeping people together
Long past the sell by date

At the core of being heard is listening.

Femme fatale
I may not be the prettiest one
The tallest one
The youngest one
The one you like or want the most
I am the one you simply can't resist
Ever

Confusion

People mostly act as if we are going to live forever
As if trust and love are finite resources
We start to be protective of them
after a major disappointment
Meanwhile life-time is the only thing
slipping away with each breath
While love and trust are limitless

Fuckboi
HURRY UP! You said
I want to get to fuck you, immediately
You're taking too long!
What do you mean you want to get to know me first
We already shared two dinners
I fed you a lobster for God's sake!
AND WAIT! You said
Wait forever, actually
To be with me
I am impatient, selfish
Insecure and emotionally unavailable
There is nothing to see here!
No promises were made
I'm just hanging out!
Like a well worn coat
With no labels on it

No one ever died a virgin.
Life fucks us all.

Revolution
The next revolution will be evolution
It will be Heaven on Earth
The next revolution
will taste and smell like a woman
Men are tired
They need rest
They need feeding
They need loving
No more violence

Love is giving total presence.

The poor of New York
You're begging
Begging for me not to leave

I'm begging
Begging for your love
I'm begging
Begging for your vicinity
I'm begging
Begging for sex
I'm begging
Begging for money
I'm begging
Begging for your time
I'm begging
Begging for your peace of mind
I'm begging
Begging for your attention
I'm begging
Begging for your thoughts
I'm begging
Begging for your approval
I'm begging
Begging for your company
I'm begging
Begging for some tenderness
I'm begging
Begging for intimacy
I'm begging
Begging for eye-contact
I'm begging
Begging for what we lost and tried to find
I'm begging
Begging for mercy

I'm begging
"I have nothing for you"
You said and threw me out
while begging for me to stay

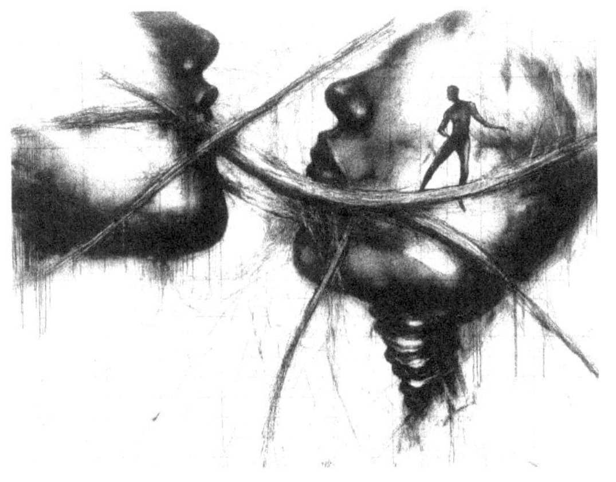

Screentime
I've never been the kind of woman
to fake orgasms
Or weakness
But you want it
You want a woman who is strong enough
to live through little death
Repeatedly
And who is weak all the same
So YOU don't have to GROW UP
Manchild
We both have to lie to one another
and ourselves to sustain this
That is why you reject the woman in the bedroom
And chase the little girls on screens
Behind the locked doors
High-pitched teenage voice….
"I've never done this before, this is my first time."
Pity
"It's normal" you tell me
But really, you mean commonplace
Your sense of shame and self-judgment tells me so
Girls becoming porn stars
Before they can legally have a sip of wine
These are your standards, not mine
Your skeletons in respectable closets
You were never more righteous
than when you were in the wrong

Love is light –
it illuminates the shadow
- within and without.

IRL

There were no streets paved with gold
To be found in New York City
But the dick is free
And shoved in your direction
Every step of the way
You know what to do
You know what you need
You know what you want
You know how it goes
It's just a fuck
Like a handshake
Or maybe less
That is how we avoid intimacy
in this Goddamn town
The distance we will go to
To avoid real touch
No one needs your middle name
It's all DTF with NSA

Blame
You never loved me
I hate you for it still
Daily
You occupy so much fucking space
Even though we no longer even are
It's awful
And I hate me for it

The depth of love will reflect the depth of grief.
For every 'new' there is letting something die.

Twilight
Sometimes I meet my shadow
At the dawn
At the window between destiny and fate
In the doorway of beginning and end
We are the ones we've been waiting for
That's all

Decisions
The most loving thing
some parents can do
for their children
is to not have them

Spring
The men boldly look you in the eye
Fearlessly devour you whole
That's how I know it's spring at last
Walking up the Bowery
When I hit 5th Avenue
A heartbeat or a two
Little Moses in red dress
I part the sea of cars passing by
Simply by my presence
They stop and wait for me to cross the street
Watching me sway in the sun
Basking in the attention
Drunk on power to stop the traffic

Jesus was a girl
Jesus was a woman
Disgraced and crucified at 33
Yes, she did come back, dead and alive
Invisible
Jesus was a woman
Rendering miracles and change
At the ultimate cost to self

If I were to have a tombstone
which I won't
It would read
"this is the only stone she left unturned".

Exquisite Inevitable

Most people are forever seeking
For dangerous safety and safe danger
The secret is to live dangerously, knowing we are safe
Because "the worst" thing that can happen is we die
And that is not so bad after all
It is the ultimate delicious certainty

A shoulder to die on
It is the curve of your shoulder that will break my neck
I think of your great big hands
Slender fingers
That won't ever be inside me again
And it sort of sucks

Crown and Bless Yourself.

Father (inheritance)
You're a gambling man
Who bet on his own folly
Trying not to lose your face
What would people think?!
The most important question…
The jovial mask hiding insecurities and hurt
You lost yourself - were you ever found?
Your father's son, addicted
Trading cards and games for teenage porn and pot
No you are not an alcoholic
You only drink sake - by the bottle
It's so sad we are destined to become our parents
We embody what damaged us the most
Can you live with it?

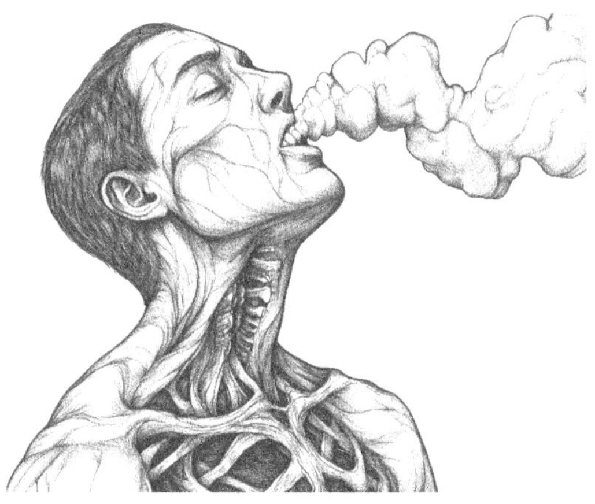

Mother (epiphany)
I had an epiphany once
In a brownstone house
In the heat of summer 2014
An old part of London off of a roundabout
in Willesden Green
Hiding naked in the garden. Sunbathing alone.
I was wearing just a huge straw hat (by Ralph Lauren)
Strawberry red
In a pair of panties
Maybe white or blue
I stepped into the living room momentarily
To get my book or lotion
And a passerby saw me through the French window
Our eyes have met
And I realised
I became my mother
Always wandering around, ogled - with Eve's innocence
Oh how this stranger loved me more than you ever could

5 years later I had another epiphany
In another house of stone
Built in 1938
I love Art Deco, especially in New York
The little building tucked away in Chelsea
Oh so neat and dear
You're screaming
I'm a cunt piece of shit. I give you nothing. I understand
nothing
Smash boom bang there goes a fist!
Through the wooden door
The furniture gets some too
The cats are terrified
I'm frozen
Frozen in time
Holy shit I became my mother

And the man inside the house hates me
I am lost

Childhood - mine and yours
Isn't it interesting how being an enigma of a character
Does not necessarily a good parent or a decent human
being make
Often rather the opposite
I cannot comprehend to this day
All the stories of your childhood - and mine
How did we survive? Maybe we didn't and this is the
aftermath
You are 3 years younger than my dad

Parents are the starting point.
Not the finishing line.

Lungs

As I've seen the Earth orbit around the Sun yet another
time
What have I learnt?
Can I breathe a little bit more freely when you are near me?
It is this newly rediscovered organ I pay attention to these
days the most
It is the one that will sustain all the other vital body parts
That get involved in the messy business of love - and its
making
LIVE. BREATHE ON

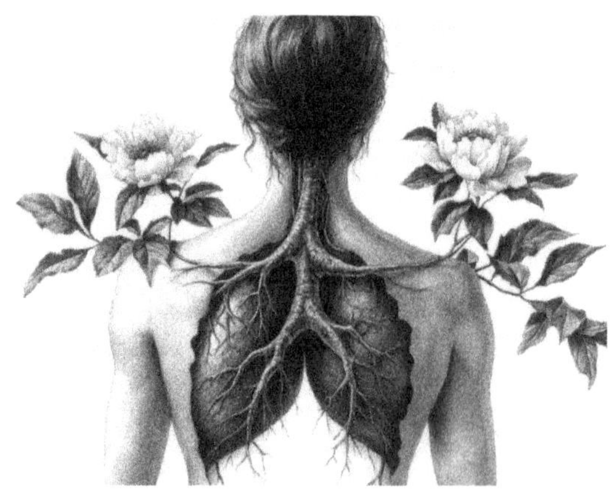

Why did we come here, where are we going?
Destiny is calling you, pulling you in the direction of
meaning.

Exit sign
In the lobby of The Ace Hotel
the fear of losing you I lost
Every exit is an entrance somewhere new